THE WHITE MATRIX

How The Trump Era Revealed

White Supremacy Is

Performance Art

A Compact Analysis of Meta-Racial Politics

in Modern America

NOVA T. LANGSTON

Copyright © 2025 RedZen Media LLC.

All rights reserved. No part of this publication may be reproduced, stored, or transmitted in any form or by any means without the prior written permission of the author.

ISBN Paperback: 979-8-218-70733-0

This book is a work of nonfiction. All opinions and interpretations are those of the author. All references to public figures are based on publicly available information and are included for purposes of commentary, criticism, or analysis. The views expressed are solely those of the author and do not represent the views of any individuals or organizations mentioned.

For business inquiries, media, or permissions, contact:

contact@thewhitematrix.com

"If you do not understand white supremacy, what it is and how it works, everything else that you think you understand will only confuse you."

— Neely Fuller Jr.

PROLOGUE

Power doesn't always shout.
Sometimes, it performs.

This is not just a book about race.
It's about the illusion around it.

White supremacy is the script.
Meta-racial politics is the stage.

The show is still running.

I've been watching it all my life.
Now I'm inviting you to watch it with me.

Table of Contents

Introduction 1

Chapter One: The Back Story 4

Chapter Two: A Classic Movie-

The White Matrix.. 10

Chapter Three: The Actors 20

Chapter Four: Drama TV Series-

The Illusion of Inclusion Era Canceled

1968-2008... 41

Chapter Five: The Real Conflict-

The Ultimate Price for Staying on Code and
Performing 48

Chapter Six: A Resolution?

The Second American Enlightenment Era.. 52

Chapter Seven: Conclusion-

A Critic's Performance Review 58

Author's Note 63

Introduction

The Trump era has revealed an unsettling truth about American society because of the profound shift in political discourse and social norms. It has exposed how deeply entrenched, yet abstract and malleable white supremacy has become. It is no longer merely a set of beliefs or an oppressive system governing social, political, economic, and racial order. It has also evolved into a form of performance art. An elaborate production built on lies, deception, and the manipulation of perception.

In this ongoing spectacle, millions participate in shaping and maintaining an alternative reality. Donald Trump (former reality TV host), his supporters, the Republican Party, and conservative media are the ones directing, producing, writing the script, and acting out the main roles in this performance. Their narrative focuses on taking America back to a time when life was simple, straight, conservative, Christian, and comfortably white. It's a fantasy in which decades of social progress have been reversed, and conservatives are shielded from liberal activist voices again. This imagined world allows supporters to ignore the many contradictions and flaws of American idealism, just like their ancestors did. It's here where racists and fascists have a safe space and white privilege won't be challenged or questioned.

The show's performances seem real and convincing and are pulling more and more Americans into this world every day. At the heart of this act is a powerful but subtle force. The shared unspoken code of white supremacy picked up by millions of Trump supporters through cultural and social influence. It's an understanding that guides people's behavior, shapes their political beliefs, and controls how they view America's identity. This code works like an invisible script, a mind synthesis among millions, creating a unified front that drives the whole manufactured illusion. This inflexible code is the core reason whites in America have dominated people of color for centuries. But it's also now the reason they are performing irrational, self-destructive behavior and tearing their country apart.

In this compact analysis, we'll dig deeper into this performance idea and its history. We'll examine how Trump supporters help build and sustain this false reality by playing their role. This isn't just the work of a small powerful group. It's a collective effort, with millions knowingly participating in a story that distorts the truth about America.

Chapter One

The BackStory

Election night in 2024 left half of America in shock. As the results came in showing Donald Trump had won again, millions couldn't believe it. How could a man who had caused an insurrection, tried to overthrow the government, and was often incompetent and corrupt be rewarded with another term? For many, it seemed like a final breakdown of American democracy.

Mainstream news pundits were struggling to make sense of it. Polls had predicted a close race or even a win for the Democrats, so they were confused by Trump's massive support. Social media exploded with reactions of outrage, disbelief, and fear, asking key questions: How did this happen again? What does this say about our country?

But for those who understand America's history with race and the system of white supremacy, the answer was clear. Trump's victories were never a fluke. It was a reflection of a long-standing truth. White supremacy isn't just an idea or an extremist hate group. It's a system built into American society that shapes laws, institutions, and social structures. And millions of Americans are willing to support it, even if it means casually discarding democracy.

To understand why Trump was able to win again, we need to look at the history that led us here. White supremacy in America was built on slavery and the oppression of people of color, yet it has always projected the illusion of a free and equal society to the world.

Historically, whenever white control has felt threatened, there has always been a backlash. After the Civil War during Reconstruction, when freed Black slaves gained rights and political power, white resistance fought back with discriminatory laws and violence. In the 1960s, when the Civil Rights Movement made progress, that resistance took on forms like mass incarceration, dog whistle politics, anti-Black political theater, and the reshaping of voter suppression.

Trump's wins didn't just come from economic struggles or angry voters. It came from a deeper fear among many white Americans feeling that their power and place in society were under attack.

A big turning point was the presidency of Barack Obama. For many Americans, Obama's election symbolized a shift where whites were no longer in charge. His time in office sparked fear and anger among those who didn't want to lose their authority. This fear led to movements like the Tea Party, which wasn't just about taxes but about race.

Trump himself fueled this fear with his birther conspiracy that claimed Obama wasn't born in the United States. When Trump officially launched his campaign in 2016, he tapped into these racial anxieties. His slogan "Make America Great Again" wasn't just about fixing the economy, it was about bringing back a time when the racial order was unquestioned.

Trump's win in 2024 showed that millions of those voters, no matter their background or education, were willing to come together again to support him. This doesn't mean every Trump supporter was a racist. But many were knowingly, and to a lesser extent unknowingly, part of a bigger system.

It is what Black author Neely Fuller Jr. talked about in his 1971 book *The United Independent Compensatory Code/System/Concept: A Compensatory Counter-Racist Code*. He speaks about the idea that the majority of whites, as a group, follow an unspoken or covert set of strict rules and practices that help maintain and perpetuate white supremacy.

Whites being "on code" means that even without directly communicating with each other, many knew what was at stake and believed Trump was their best chance to uphold their dominance. This code was set into motion the moment Trump descended the escalator at Trump Tower and announced his presidential bid.

His racist rhetoric against immigrants was a signal to millions of Americans who shared his views. It was an open dog whistle and rallying cry for those who believed in preserving the white power structure. This cast Trump as a mythical white savior figure, whom his supporters believed was sent by God to save America from the "threat" of racial equality.

The alliance was forged, and loyalty to Trump became mandatory in the conservative movement. This code amongst millions of whites won him his first presidential term, which led to policies like immigration bans, appointing ultra-conservative judges, and attacking "woke" culture.

For many voters, supporting Trump wasn't just about politics, it was about protecting their place against America's changing demographics. More immigration, more racial diversity, and the political power of nonwhite communities were scary to many Americans.

The idea that white people could lose their majority status in the country felt like a threat. Instead of embracing this change, many of those voters chose a radical president to execute a radical agenda. From attacking Black Lives Matter, to banning Muslims, to separating families at the border, Trump immediately began taking extreme actions to push back against diversity and social justice movements.

Trump's triumphs also revealed how white supremacy expands beyond just policies. It's about controlling the audience's thoughts and perception of reality. Millions of Americans were willing to ignore Trump's crimes and corruption because they were deeply invested in an illusion of *The Rebirth Of A Past Great America* that he pitched to them.

In the next chapters, we'll explore how this illusion is built and maintained. We'll also look at examples of how manipulative lies, contradictions and media propaganda shape America's worldview, ensuring the performance of racial power continues.

Chapter Two

A Classic Movie:

The White Matrix

Have you ever felt like you're living in a fake world, with fake people, where nothing seems real and everything feels like an illusion? Kind of like in the 1999 movie *The Matrix*, where people live in a computer-generated world without knowing it.

Well, you're not too far off. You're not in a computer-simulated reality, you're in a human one. You are living in a world that's been carefully controlled by a system that manipulates what you see, hear, and believe. That simulated reality is called *The White Matrix*.

From the moment you're born, this matrix starts working on your mind. It starts small, with positive images and ideas about whiteness being the norm in the things you see, like baby toys, coloring books, and TV shows which build racial trust. As you grow, the media you consume and the history you learn all support the idea that white dominance is natural and permanent. Those in power don't need to force their views on you. They've already planted the seeds in your mind, shaping how you see the world and suppressing any ideas that challenge that view. They control what is real and what is not.

In *The Trump Era*, reality itself has become something people fight over. It's no longer just about politics. It's about how people see and understand the world.

The White Matrix is a system of performance where millions who believe in upholding white supremacy at all cost, are working together to control what we believe to be true. This effort to manipulate reality isn't just happening in conservative news and social media spaces. It's happening in everyday life, with regular people supporting this system. You have interactions with them at your job, the grocery stores, and the doctor's office.

We will symbolize this group as the 57 Percenters, a reference to exit polls that revealed 57% of the white majority supported Trump's re-election, even in the face of overwhelming evidence of his felony convictions, corruption, incompetence, authoritarian ambition, and the role in the January 6 insurrection. This was the metaphorical Rubicon that millions of these voters chose to cross. It revealed a harsh truth. America's racial institution was more sacred than the Constitution itself.

These 57 Percenters are performing around you every day. They're on your TV, at your neighborhood festivals, liking your social media posts and cheering for your kids at a soccer game. Some are your friends, acquaintances, and co-workers. You have friendly and close relationships with them, but behind the mask, they will uphold white supremacy at all costs at your expense. Because deep inside their minds, 57 Percenters don't see the oppression of people of color as right or wrong. They're indifferent and quietly understand that it is a necessary moral concession to preserve the system.

The 57 Percenters are not racist mindless drones. They are self-aware, strategic, and highly coordinated, even when they do not communicate directly. Their ability to operate in unison without public direction is a result of cultural osmosis and a shared understanding of the necessity to maintain the status quo. The power does not come from open declarations of white supremacy but from their ability to manipulate perception. And controlling the narrative and making the world believe whatever they want it to believe is their greatest weapon.

Weaponizing Language:

The Hijacking of "Woke"

One of the clearest examples of this manipulation is the way the 57 Percenters have twisted the meaning of words to suit their agenda. The term "woke" once had a positive and straightforward meaning. It referred to a state of being aware of social injustices, particularly racial injustice. It was a term rooted in Black activism, an encouragement to be conscious of oppression and systemic inequality.

However, the 57 Percenters saw the potential power in the term and worked systematically to distort its meaning. Right-wing media outlets, conservative politicians, and online influencers all engaged in a coordinated effort to redefine "woke" as something negative. They associated it with extremism, absurdity, and even tyranny. They framed it as a threat to traditional values, using it as a catch-all insult for anything that challenged white supremacy or promoted diversity. In just a few years, the original meaning of "woke" was nearly erased from mainstream discourse and replaced by the 57 Percenter definition.

This is a perfect example of how *The White Matrix* operates. The 57 Percenters did not simply argue against woke culture. They rewrote reality itself. They convinced millions of Americans, including some moderates and liberals, that "woke" was something to be feared and opposed, even when they could not define what it meant. This was not accidental. It was a deliberate manipulation tactic of perception, designed to ensure that social progress was demonized and that the fight for racial justice was dismissed as irrational extremism.

Controlling Perception:

The Rigged Election Lie

Another prime example of *The White Matrix* in action is the false narrative surrounding election fraud. When Donald Trump lost the 2020 election, he immediately claimed that the election had been stolen from him. There was no evidence of widespread fraud, and every legal challenge brought forth by his team failed. And yet, millions of Trump supporters got on code, repeating the lie over and over again until it became a reality within their ecosystem.

Through conservative media, social media influencers, and elected officials, the lie was cemented into the collective consciousness of conservatives. Despite all evidence to the contrary, millions believed it without question. And more importantly, they acted on it. Republican-led states began passing restrictive voting laws, citing a fraud that never happened. The mere act of repeating the lie enough times allowed them to reshape reality itself, creating new laws, new policies, and a new political landscape based on something entirely fabricated.

This is how *The White Matrix* functions. The 57 Percenters do not need evidence or logic. They simply need to stick to their narrative and repeat it with enough conviction until the broader society begins to question its own understanding of reality. If they want the sky to be green, they will insist on it relentlessly until people begin to doubt their own eyes. This is not ignorance. It is performance, an intentional strategy to create confusion and disorient those who would otherwise resist their agenda.

The Team Effort to Enforce the Narrative

The strength of *The White Matrix* is that it is a team effort. Millions of 57 Percenters understand their role in maintaining the illusion, even if they do not explicitly articulate it. When Trump lies, conservative media outlets reinforce it. When right-wing politicians enact policies based on those lies, right-wing judges uphold them. When white suburban parents panic over manufactured culture war issues, school boards, police departments, and local governments all align to push policies that reinforce those fears.

There is no central command issuing orders. Instead, there is a shared understanding among 57 Percenters that they must stick to the lie, no matter what. The moment they break rank and acknowledge the truth, the illusion collapses, and the power they hold over perception begins to weaken. This is why you rarely see Republican politicians openly contradict Trump, even when they know he is lying. It is why conservative media personalities who used to criticize Trump eventually fell in line. They understand that in *The White Matrix*, perception is more important than reality, and to break from the collective lie is to betray the system itself.

The Broader Implications:

Living in The White Matrix

The manipulation of perception does not just impact politics. It shapes how society functions at every level.

From education to criminal justice, from entertainment to corporate policies, *The White Matrix* ensures that whiteness remains the default and that challenges to the status quo are neutralized. It is why police brutality against Black Americans is excused, and why white mass shooters are humanized while Black victims are demonized. And why systemic racism is dismissed as a myth even as its effects are clearly visible.

By controlling narratives, the 57 Percenters ensure that even when white supremacy is not explicitly enforced through laws, it is still deeply ingrained in the way society operates. They do not need to say "white people are superior." They simply need to shape reality in a way that ensures white people remain in positions of power and control.

Breaking Free: Recognizing The White Matrix for What It Is

The first step in resisting *The White Matrix* is recognizing it for what it is. It is a deliberate, coordinated effort to manipulate perception and uphold the status quo at any cost. It is not simply a matter of ignorance or political disagreement. It is a systemic performance designed to control how we see the world. Understanding this framework allows us to see through the lies, to call out the performance for what it is, and to push back against the narratives that seek to distort reality.

The Trump Era has revealed *The White Matrix* for clear view. The question moving forward is, how do we disrupt it? How do we challenge a system where truth and reality itself are constantly under attack?

That is the battle ahead, and it will require a level of awareness and resistance that goes beyond simply calling out lies. It requires dismantling the structures that allow these deceptions to flourish in the first place.

The White Matrix is real. It's in your face every day. The question is, can Americans see beyond it and break free?

Chapter Three

The Actors

The White Matrix is a domineering mindset that millions of Americans perform every day. It's not just the extremists or openly racist people. It's also regular folks like politicians, churchgoers, teachers, and everyday citizens. These people play specific "roles" in keeping the system of white supremacy going, often without even saying a word. They've learned how things are "supposed to be," and they stick to those rules to help maintain the status quo. There's no need for formal organizations. This system runs on learned behaviors and cultural reinforcement. Everyone has their part to play in this big performance.

There are several key archetypes that help keep the show going. Here are a few:

The Christian Actor:

Hiding Behind Morality

The *Christian Actor* is someone who uses religion to justify harmful beliefs, especially around race. They loudly proclaim their Christian values but ignore Jesus' teachings about love, compassion, and justice when it comes to racial equality. This group overwhelmingly supported Trump despite his actions being fundamentally opposite to what they claim to believe. That's because *Christian Actors* believe what's right and wrong is subjective. Their religion is the preservation of white Christian dominance which is less about faith and more about allegiance. It's a belief system, complete with rituals, loyalty tests, and unquestioned doctrine.

The Patriot Actor:

Defending Oppression as Tradition

The *Patriot Actor* is someone who claims to love America and its Constitution but supports policies that undermine democracy. They shout about freedom, but only for people who look and think like them. When racial minorities fight for their rights, they suddenly become authoritarian, pushing for voter suppression and police violence. We saw this in action during the January 6th Capitol riot, when people who claimed to support democracy tried to overthrow an election. The *Patriot Actor* wants to return to a time when white dominance was unquestioned, and "Make America Great Again" is coded language for wanting things to go back to that time.

The Liar Actor:

Manufacturing False Narratives

The *Liar Actor* spreads lies to shape how people see reality. These actors are often politicians, social media influencers, and media figures who deliberately twist the truth about history and current events. They deny things like slavery's impact or the existence of systemic racism. One of the most famous *Liar Actors* is Donald Trump himself, who built a political movement based on lies, like claiming Obama wasn't born in the U.S. or falsely claiming the 2020 election was stolen. These lies are spread by regular people too through social media and word of mouth.

The Gaslighter Actor:

Rewriting Reality in Real-Time

The *Gaslighter Actor* works to make others doubt their own experiences. They tell people that racism doesn't exist, even when there's clear evidence to the contrary. When police brutality is caught on video, they change the subject to something unrelated, like "Black-on-Black crime." When the effects of systemic racism are pointed out, they brush it off by saying things like, "That was a long time ago. You weren't a slave. Get over it." Their goal is to confuse and make people feel like their experiences aren't real, that it's just a figment of their imagination or insignificant.

The Projectionist Actor:

Accusing Others of Their Own Crimes

The *Projectionist Actor* accuses others of the things they are guilty of themselves. They flip the narrative by projecting their own bigotry, fear, or hostility onto the people pushing for justice.

For example, they might call anti-racists "the real racists," or say that efforts to make society more equal and diverse are attempts to destroy white people. When Trump incites far-right violence, his supporters accuse Democrats of tearing the country apart. When white mass shooters commit senseless murders, the *Projectionist Actor* shifts the blame to mental health, deflecting attention away from racial hatred.

The Playing Dumb Actor:

Feigned Ignorance as a Strategy

Sometimes, white supremacy is maintained not through direct aggression, but through pretending not to understand. The *Playing Dumb Actor* acts like they don't get racism, even when it's explained clearly. They're responses are always, "Why is everything about race?" or "Aren't we all just Americans?" They use this act of ignorance to avoid acknowledging racial injustice, pretending that it's too complicated to understand, even though they can grasp other complex topics just fine. The *Playing Dumb Actor* knows that the racial problems in society will never be solved as long as they keep pretending they don't understand them, so they will continue to perform ignorance into infinity.

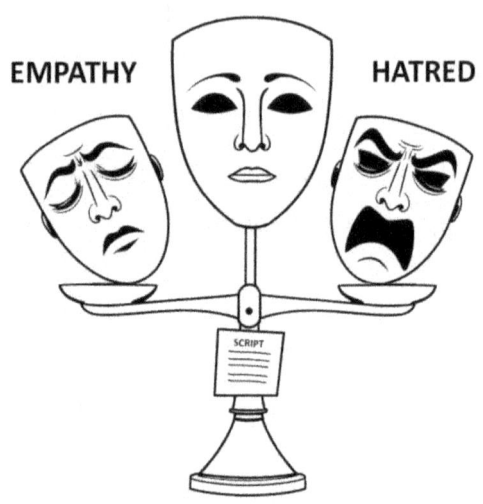

The Moderate Actor:

The Passive Enabler

The *Moderate Actor* claims to support equality but never takes a real stand. They'll say they're against racism, but when it comes to real-world issues, they stay silent. Instead of taking a position, they push for "both sides" arguments, trying to appear neutral, even when one side is clearly right and the other clearly wrong. Fearful of being targeted or alienated from their own race for getting off code, they play it safe. They're fine with diversity, but only if it doesn't challenge their own comfort or privilege.

The Reverse Racism Victim Actor:

Flipping the Script

The *Reverse Racism Victim Actor* believes that white people are the real victims of racism. They claim things like affirmative action is discrimination against white people, or that saying "Black Lives Matter" means that white lives don't. This role is used to stop progress in its tracks. By pretending that they're the ones being oppressed, they try to derail conversations about racial justice and stop any change from happening.

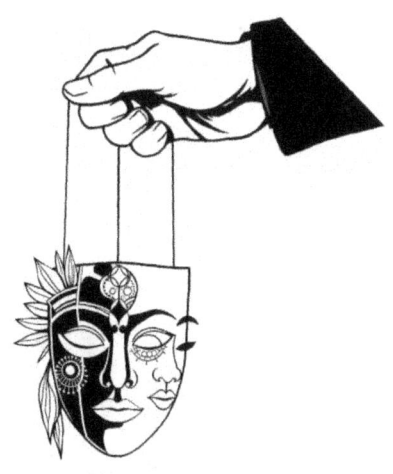

The Minority Collaborator Actor:

Selling Out for Acceptance

Some nonwhite people, like Black, Latino, Asian and others play the role of the *Minority Collaborator Actor*. These people align themselves with white supremacy, often out of internalized racism or as a means of personal advancement. Liberal media critics often mention public figures like Candace Owens as a high profile example. They fill the role as spokespersons or "tokens" for the system that oppresses their people, proving that white supremacy rewards those who betray their own. The *Minority Collaborator Actor* tends to over-perform because they crave white acceptance and want to show their allegiance to the system.

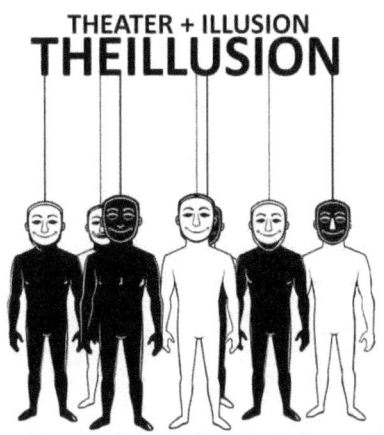

theillusion *(noun)-A constructed social or psychological reality that operates like a performance, where dominant powers script, stage, and sustain illusions to control perception, behavior & belief.*

A Carefully Choreographed Performance

Every person who plays one of these roles helps keep white supremacy active. Whether it's an internet troll gaslighting you with bad faith or circular arguments. Or a "Karen" playing victim, instantly triggering tears after instigating a racial conflict. Or a cable news pundit rationalizing Trump's destructive behavior as normal, they're all performing mental gymnastics in *The White Matrix*. They twist reality to maintain the idea that white people are always right and in control. The first step to breaking free from this system is recognizing the performance for what it is, and exposing it for what it's doing.

But how do we stop the show?

Chapter Four

Drama TV Series:

The Illusion of Inclusion Era Canceled

1968-2008

The Civil Rights Movement of the 1950s and 1960s forced white America to confront the realities of its racist past. And the assassination of Dr. Martin Luther King Jr. in 1968 underscored the urgency of the moment. Demands for justice, equality, and the dismantling of white supremacy could no longer be ignored. However, instead of responding with the same kind of brutal racism defined in the past Jim Crow era, America shifted tactics. A new performance strategy emerged, one that gave the appearance of progress while keeping the foundational structures of racial inequality intact.

This period, from the late 1960s to Barack Obama's election in 2008, is called *The Illusion of Inclusion Era*.

During this time, Black visibility increased significantly in spaces like media, politics, sports, and corporate leadership.

Political figures like Shirley Chisholm, the first Black woman elected to Congress in 1968, and Jesse Jackson, who ran for president in the 1980s, broke barriers and inspired hope. In entertainment, Black celebrities became increasingly mainstream. Richard Pryor dominated comedy in the 1970s. *The Cosby Show* in the 1980s depicted an upper-middle-class Black family that was the highest-rated TV sitcom of the decade. In sports, in the 1990s, Michael Jordan became the most marketable and famous athlete in the world. These images helped reinforce the idea that racism was fading, and that inclusion was real. But these were notable exceptions, not indicators of systemic transformation.

Instead of white supremacy using laws and violence to keep Blacks excluded like in the past, symbolic Black representation became the new tool of control. America started putting Black individuals in visible positions of power and privilege to give the illusion of progress.

At the same time, the criminal justice system was moving in the opposite direction. The War on Drugs, started by President Nixon in the 1970s, expanded under Reagan in the 1980s, and escalated under Clinton in the 1990s, disproportionately targeted Black Americans. Sentencing laws punished crack cocaine in Black communities far more harshly than powder cocaine used in white communities, showing how the legal system was still strategically being used to criminalize Black existence.

As Michelle Alexander argues in her book *The New Jim Crow*, mass incarceration became the new mechanism for racial control. It replaced the old Jim Crow laws with a more quiet but equally destructive system.

So while white supremacy was pushing more Black Americans into being more visible in culture and politics, millions were being pushed out of society through mass incarceration. This contradiction centers *The Illusion of Inclusion Era* clearly. Black representation may have increased, but equity didn't follow and the visibility shown can never be mistaken for justice.

Another foundational piece of this illusion was the structural prevention of Blacks building economic power in their communities. While a small percentage of Black Americans achieved financial success, the majority continued to face significant economic barriers.

The racial wealth gap, rooted in slavery, persisted well into the 1960s and beyond. Programs like affirmative action opened some doors to white-collar jobs, but it didn't fundamentally shift the broader economic landscape. Many Black neighborhoods remained neglected and underfunded. Their families were blocked from fair loans and their children were sent to poor schools. This was by design. In 1984, the median wealth of white families was twelve times that of Black families, and by 2009 it had widened to eighteen times.

This growing divide was no accident. It reflected generations of systemic exclusion from homeownership, education, and equal wages. And while representation in media, politics, and business improved, it often served to mask the deeper structures that continued to block real economic mobility for most Black Americans.

A Different Type of TV Star

The illusion that America had moved beyond race was shattered in 2008 with the election of Barack Obama. Many people thought his victory meant that Martin Luther King Jr.'s dream had come true and that America was "post-racial." But this was never the case. The backlash to Obama's presidency showed just how fragile the illusion was.

Immediately, racist conspiracy theories about Obama spread, and a white nationalist and Tea Party movement emerged, driven by fear that a Black president symbolized the decline of white power. Obama's election marked the beginning of the end of *The Illusion of Inclusion Era* because the strong racial tension underneath the surface started exploding.

While some believed America had moved beyond its racist past, the violent reaction to Obama, and the rise of Donald

Trump, showed that white supremacy was still the country's core power structure.

What It All Means

The Illusion of Inclusion Era was never about real racial progress. It was about making enough changes on the surface to make it look like things were improving while making sure whites stayed in control. The visibility of Black people in media, politics, and corporate America didn't mean systemic change. It was a carefully managed performance to make America feel like it was improving when, the truth is, nothing had really changed. The response from conservative America was quick and harsh after Obama was elected president because the illusion had gone too far. And the rise in police violence, white nationalism, anti-Black hate crimes, and attacks on social justice movements like Black Lives Matter was the result.

The reality is that *The Trump Era* brought the final curtain down on *The Illusion of Inclusion Era*, exposing the myth of racial progress. Now in its place, a new script is being written. A *New Modern Jim Crow Era* is in the works and this show will rely less on performance and more on bold, unapologetic white cruelty and control. This era will also be coupled with unchecked billionaire greed and corruption.

The system will be laid bare, and exposed for all to see and understand. So now the questions become, what role will we play? Do we challenge the script, or let the next act of oppression unfold as planned? This era will more than likely lead to the American Empire's collapse. Only one true answer can be given with certainty at this time.

We will need help from those in the 57 percent to break free from *The White Matrix* to save America from destruction.

Chapter Five

The Real Conflict:

The Ultimate Price for Staying on Code and Performing

While white supremacy has always been at the core of America's social order, a new order is emerging. The unchecked power of billionaires and corporate elites. America is becoming an oligarchy, meaning the wealthiest people are gaining more control over politics, the media, and government policies. Trump's tax cuts and pro-business policies will mainly benefit the rich while taking away protections for the working class. His economic policies will push America further into a dangerous divide between the top 1% and everyone else.

But even though poor and working-class whites will be hurt, many will still stay on code and perform for Trump. Why? Because, like in the past, they've chosen to have a fellowship with wealthy whites in power rather than stand with people of color even when their economic and political interests align.

In the past, the ruling class invented the concept of race as a way to divide poor people. Ever since the 1600s, they gave poor whites small privileges over blacks to keep them from uniting. This tactic was used during the Jim Crow era as well and is still happening today. Trump, Republicans, Fox News and other right-wing media outlets stoke fear and anger among whites, encouraging them to blame blacks, immigrants, and liberals for their problems, rather than acknowledging the wealthy elites who are truly responsible for their suffering.

As a consequence, issues like rural hospitals closing, opioid addiction, and stagnating wages in white communities will only worsen. Public services, education, and healthcare will be cut also. As economic hardship intensifies, race will be increasingly used as a tool to distract from the real culprits, the rich elites and the corrupt system that sustains them.

Eventually, this oppressive system will reach a breaking point and a mix of economic collapse, racial tensions, and reckless right-wing media propaganda will explode in political violence and civil unrest.

So, we have more questions to add. Will poor and working-class whites finally realize they've been tricked into being loyal to a system that isn't loyal to them? Or will they stay on code with white supremacy just to hold on to their minor white privileges? Will they wake up and quit performing in *The White Matrix* and join forces with people of color to challenge the real power? Or will they stick to their racial loyalty and continue supporting policies that hurt them and hurt us? Only time will tell.

But, there could still be hope in the fallout of *The Trump Era's* atomic disaster, Americans will grow desperate for answers and slowly begin to seek sanity once again. It won't be an immediate or universal shift, but over time, some individuals will see through the lies and start demanding accountability.

And as a result, maybe poor and working-class whites will finally grasp that their loyalty to race won't pay their bills or help their families. They'll see that the rich elites they've been supporting don't care about their survival, they only want their money and obedience. Some will break free from the matrix, while others will continue down the path of extreme white nationalism. But eventually, the illusion that white supremacy benefits them will fall apart.

Chapter Six

A Resolution?

The Second American Enlightenment Era

The voting data of the 2024 presidential election revealed a sobering reality. Only 30% of Americans could see past the lies and illusions and fully comprehend what was right in front of them. Nothing had changed, Trump was still a clear threat to democracy and the country's stability. But even after eight years of erratic unhinged behavior that was broadcast daily, 70% of Americans cast their vote for Trump to extend the chaos or didn't vote at all. It's a damning reflection of a nation blinded by hate, greed, apathy or too intellectually lazy to inform themselves with the truth. We are driving on a self-destructive path, and Trump's second term will only accelerate it.

But even in these challenging times, Americans could find reason for some inspiration by understanding history and looking to the European Enlightenment of the past. An era born from conflict, defined by intellectual rebellion, and marked by sweeping political change.

History has shown us that when empires become too proud, corrupt, and socially and economically unbalanced, they eventually collapse. The United States seems to be following a similar trajectory. Under Trump and his billionaire allies, the widening gap between the rich and the poor is beginning to mirror the conditions that triggered past revolutions. The growing inequality, the erosion of truth, and the manipulation of public perception all echo the pre-revolutionary climate of late 18th-century France.

Back then, France was a global power ruled by an elite class that was out of touch, who lived lavishly while the majority suffered. The monarchy maintained its grip through propaganda and fear, convincing the poor that their misery was fate and that resistance was pointless.

However, the Enlightenment in France sparked a shift in thinking and ignited a demand for change. America's wealthy elite use similar tactics, controlling narratives through biased media, corporate influence, and culture wars. We can easily draw parallels between that historic period and the present. The American poor and working class, today's modern-day peasants and commoners, could become enlightened or "woke" in the truest sense.

This is why a new era of Enlightenment in America can be possible. One rooted in critical thinking and a commitment to shared truth. Americans would be awakened to the reality that the system is rigged by wealthy elites, much like monarchs and nobles of the past. Through the power of thought and not violence, we could begin to demand a fairer, more equitable society.

For some among the 57 Percenters, it may take hitting rock bottom before racial pride and stubborn denial begin to waiver. Only then, disillusioned Americans exhausted by lies and division, begin to rediscover reason, common purpose, and the strength found in unity. As illusions fade and the machinery of deception breaks down, people may begin to see the world as it truly is. And from the ruins of the post-Trump era, a Second American Enlightenment could arise, one defined by awakening, renewal, and genuine progress.

It won't be rooted in hashtags or outrage, but in clarity, consciousness, and a social intellectual revolution. We could call it, perhaps, a New Woke Era?

The New Woke Era

In *The White Matrix* the term "woke" has long been used as a tool to push back against diversity, equity, and inclusion (DEI). It has been weaponized as a catch-all insult to undermine decades of social and political progress, often reducing complex issues to simplistic soundbites. A word twisted to label those advocating for racial and social justice as overzealous or out of touch, serving as a tool to halt meaningful change.

But in this new era, reclaiming "woke" could be a powerful act of resistance. It could be redefined not as a pejorative, but as a commitment to waking up from the illusions that have kept America divided. It would mean confronting uncomfortable truths about systemic racism, economic inequality, and social, environmental destruction, and taking action to address them.

In *The New Woke Era*, we could shift the focus back to what it truly means to be awake, which is to be alert and aware of the deeper societal issues that have long been ignored or minimized. This would be a time when people no longer fall for the distractions and manipulations that kept them divided. Instead, we could strive for collective understanding and start with a focus on inclusivity, honesty and justice. *The New Woke Era* would be about expanding our vision of what is possible and working together to create a more equitable and enlightened future.

Media will change too. More people will demand accurate, objective news and reject the false narratives pushed by profit-driven news media and right-wing outlets. While disinformation will still be strong because of its profitability, it will begin to lose its grip as more people wake up to the truth. The movement for economic and racial justice will grow as more people realize they don't want to live in a country run by greedy billionaires and cruel white nationalists. The next few years will decide if America follows the path of other fallen empires or if it can change course before collapsing completely.

The New Woke Era will not come easily. Many people will fight to keep things the way they are, clinging to old racial hierarchies and authoritarian control. But for those willing to face the truth, the post-Trump era offers a chance to rebuild a society grounded in reality, facts, science, empathy, and human dignity again.

Chapter Seven

Conclusion:

A Critic's Performance Review

America stands at a crossroads, caught in a struggle between two opposing forces. The classic system of white supremacy versus the growing awareness that the illusions of this system can no longer hold the country together. *The Trump Era* didn't invent this conflict, it only made it more obvious, turning it into a full-blown spectacle. A spectacle without limits, a political circus fueled by chaos and corruption, determined to protect racial dominance at any cost.

Throughout this compact analysis, we've explored how white supremacy isn't just structural, it's psychological and theatrical. A performance that shapes perception. That system of performance is called *The White Matrix*. The actors include everybody from media talking heads, businessmen, and politicians to everyday people. *The*

White Matrix thrives on manipulation and false narratives, but systems built on lies eventually collapse.

The Trump Era forces many Americans to confront the uncomfortable truth about their country. For years, liberals, moderates, and even some conservatives thought America was slowly moving toward a more open-minded equal society. Obama's election was seen as proof that the country had overcome its racist past or was at least going in the right direction.

However, the backlash to Obama led to Trump's presidency which destroyed that racially inclusive illusion. We've seen consistently in *The Trump Era*, that the idea of endless American greatness, white superiority, and conservative values has crumbled under the weight of its own contradictions. Millions who claimed to believe in democracy and law and order, turned their backs on those values to remain loyal to a fascist reality TV star. The 57 Percenters didn't vote for policy or country, they voted to protect a racial institution, even if it meant burning their country down.

Yet, even in this time of social dysfunction, shameless lies, and alternate realities, cracks are starting to show. More people are asking why policies that hurt working-class people are supported by those who claim to be their advocates. More Americans, especially younger ones, are rejecting the narratives pushed by conservative media and politicians. The constant outrage over things like "woke culture" and "reverse racism" is being exposed as deceptive distractions.

Americans are also mentally and spiritually drained from years of an environment of relentless hate, fear, anger, and divisiveness that Trump built. It's a metaphorical poison. The human soul can only endure so much negativity before it develops a desperate hunger for something more positive and peaceful.

This is why I believe a new Enlightenment era is coming. For *The New Woke Era* to begin, there must be a collective awakening. Minds must be sparked with curiosity and questions about how the real world works. Only then can people begin to break free from the illusions they've been brainwashed by, and see the systems shaping their lives for what they really are.

People need to reject the lies and falsehoods that have defined *The Trump Era*. Poor and working-class white Americans must see that their true adversaries are not immigrants or people of color but the wealthy elites who have always exploited them. This means the majority of Americans must choose solidarity over division, facts over lies, reality over illusion, democracy over authoritarianism. And ultimately, we must confront and dismantle the system of white supremacy that has shaped this nation from the very beginning.

So, in conclusion, *The Trump Era* has revealed white supremacy as performance art, one in which millions of people play their roles to maintain an illusion to uphold white dominance at all cost. The final question is: will Americans finally snap out of *The White Matrix*, or will they continue to perform as America descends further into self-destruction?

The stage is set. The actors are in place. The final act is about to begin.

The choice is ours.

Author's Note

Thank you for taking the time to step into this world, a space where we strive to see things as they truly are. Here, critical thinking lays the foundation. Reality forms the frame. Truth builds the walls.

This house had to be built because more than half of America kept telling me not to use my brain, to ignore my own eyes and ears. I was told not to ask questions, not to think, just to accept whatever I was given and smile.

That's why this book exists. It's a brief exploration of history, and a deeper look at the illusions that have shaped the American landscape.

I wrote this for those who feel confused, those trying to make sense of the constant lies and contradictions around us. So many have been emotionally bound to these illusions for so long, they can no longer recognize what's real and what's not.

That's why I believe in the power of language, to challenge, to reveal, and to guide. If this book helps you navigate a little clearer, think a little deeper, or move a little freer, then it's done its job.

— Nova T. Langston

www.ingramcontent.com/pod-product-compliance
Lightning Source LLC
Chambersburg PA
CBHW060703030426
42337CB00017B/2745